Praise for *40 Things to Teach Your Children Before You Die*

"Obedience is simple, rationalization complicated. Gregg Jackson takes us back to the simple things, calling us to submit to the wisdom of the God who made us. Read the book; take it to heart; teach it to your children. They will thank you, as will your grandchildren."

–Dr. R.C. Sproul, Jr., professor, Reformation Bible
College, pastor, Ascension Presbyterian Church

"The 40 lessons that Gregg Jackson wants to teach his children (that the secular world won't) are not only undeniably biblical, but they are unapologetically orthodox; they are not only filled with a realistic worldview of Creation-Fall, but also a glorious hope of Christ-centered Redemption; and, most importantly, not just for children, but for all of us. We need this today because, increasingly, tragically, many in the evangelical world (and other conservative Christian communities) will not teach these truths. Our twenty-year-old 'baby' is studying history at university in Britain. I guarantee you: I will be posting this across the pond to him as soon as I can! So, I commend it to the Church without reservation. The author and publisher deserve our gratitude."

–Michael A. Milton, PhD, author, musician,
President and Senior Fellow, D. James Kennedy Institute
for Christianity and Culture; Fourth President-Chancellor,
Reformed Theological Seminary

"Your children are a sacred trust from God to you. You have a divine responsibility to impart in them truths that society, media, and the educational system will not teach them. Gregg Jackson has identified forty key truths that parents need to teach their children. Tragically, nine out of ten children from evangelical homes walk away from their faith by the time they enter college. One of the biggest reasons for that is that their parents did not impart in their children a truly biblical worldview. Gregg has simplified the process and has prioritized key areas that can transform your children's view of themselves and the world. This book is a very powerful tool for parents to use! I encourage you to get Gregg's book and use those tools and watch your child's life become something beautiful and powerful for God!"

–Paul McGuire, bestselling author and speaker

"This book has great potential for the discipleship of our youth and school-age children. As a short Q-and-A book, it deals with many of the important worldview issues in which our children need to be equipped, such as creation versus evolution. Easy to read, and with good concise arguments and scriptural support, this book is needed in the family and Christian schools. It is useful for children in public school as well, to offset the negative indoctrination. Good for family worship and bedtime instruction for children as well. I heartily recommend this outstanding book!"

–E. Ray Moore, Chaplain, (Lt. Col.) USAR (Ret.); President, Frontline Ministries, Inc. and Exodus Mandate

"Gregg Jackson nails it again! Gregg is a skilled communicator, and in *40 Things to Teach Your Children Before You Die*, he once again demonstrates his ability to 'cut to the chase' in dealing with the stuff of life and faith that truly matters. What a beautifully powerful presentation of these eternal biblical truths. Make certain you get several copies; this is a book you will want to share with others!"

–Carl Gallups, bestselling author, radio and
TV host, and Senior Pastor, Hickory Hammock
Baptist Church (Milton, Florida)

"I think Gregg's book *40 Things to Teach Your Children Before You Die* will enable Christian parents to help inoculate their kids from the lies and propaganda of the godless educational system and culture at large and help them to think and act biblically."

–J.C. Watts, former U.S. Congressman (Oklahoma)

"Gregg Jackson has done it again. From the Conservative-Book-of-the-Month selection, and then to the Book-of-the-Year selection, Gregg has now written a book that every parent and grandparent should read! And those of us with younger kids should read *40 Things to Teach Your Children Before You Die* to them out loud!"

–Bob Enyart, Senior Pastor, Denver Bible Church; radio
host of Bob Enyart Live and Real Science Friday

"Gregg Jackson has done something King David demonstrated as true wisdom long ago. I call it *generational thinking*. This Hebrew King, who achieved a heart just like his God, wrote, 'So teach us to number our days, that we may apply our hearts unto wisdom' (Psalm 90:1). Gregg has embraced his mortality and responded by passing along immortal truths to his children and yours. May we all be as wise. I commend this to your reading."

–Cary K. Gordon, Executive Pastor,
Cornerstone World Outreach

"I absolutely love this book! It's great for kids, but is also wonderful for grown-ups. The information in this book reminded me of the basics of salvation... and clarified the truth of the Gospel in terms that both children and adults can simply and factually understand. When it is published, I will buy several to give to my grandchildren and my adult children, plus friends. In our everyday lives, we forget the basics of the truths you have in the book, and it brings us right back to the simple realities of salvation; plus it gently clarifies the facts regarding the misinformation that is taught in our schools, and in all stages of our lives."

–Tricia Erickson, author;
President of Angel Pictures and Publicity

"*40 Things to Teach Your Children Before You Die* is a comprehensive yet easy read, presenting the key points of a biblical Christian worldview for parents to train up their children in the way they should go. Gregg's book is recommended reading for caring Christian parents. Gregg Jackson is on a mission from God to redeem the culture. His words and works have Grace and Providential Power. I am honored to call him a friend."

—Dr. Ted Baehr, President, Movieguide

"In our day and age, when life is a status update on Facebook or a tweet in 140 characters or less, it's tough to be both purposeful and pithy, but Gregg Jackson has found that necessary niche with this worthwhile read. The points addressed in this book ought to be standard discussion topics in every Christian home in America."

—Steve Deace, author and nationally syndicated radio host

"Gregg Jackson has used his pen to pierce the veil of Satan's most powerful plan to destroy humanity. That plan is to remove the truth of God and His Word from our youth. This book is a last will and testament to save humanity."

—Pastor James David Manning, Atlah World Ministries

"In a time when lies seem to rule the day, Gregg Jackson cuts through the fog and crystallizes for us the truths that were once known as *common sense*. Sadly, today in America, *sense* is no longer *common*, but is an opinion. The issues that Gregg deals with in his book are essential building blocks upon which we can stand in our efforts to restore sanity to a morally confused nation."

—Coach Dave Daubenmire, radio host and speaker,
Pass The Salt Ministries

"Have you ever wondered the type of lessons you should be passing along to your kids? Sure you have. We all have. My friend Gregg Jackson has given us all a plan in *40 Things to Teach Your Kids Before You Die*. After more than two decades of working with kids and parents, I can confidently say that this is the most simple, truthful, systematic resource I have seen for parents wanting to disciple their own sons and daughters."

–Greg Davis, President, First Priority of Birmingham, Alabama (America's largest city-wide campus ministry organization); host, *Priority Talk Live Christian Radio*

"Gregg has produced a wonderful, timely resource. More than ever before, our youth need to hear and defend *truth* according to God's Word. Someone once said, 'Children are the message we will send to a generation we will not see.' This book will help impact future generations in a positive way."

–Robyn Carnes, Elementary Chaplain, Cherry Hills Christian School

40 Things to Teach Your Children Before You Die

The Simple American Truths about Life, Family, and Faith
(That the World Won't Teach Them)

GREGG JACKSON
Best Selling Author

DUNHAM
books

Contents

Dedication

"My son [Jake], do not let wisdom and understanding out of your sight, preserve sound judgment and discretion; they will be life for you, an ornament to grace your neck. Then you will go on your way in safety, and your foot will not stumble. When you lie down, you will not be afraid; when you lie down, your sleep will be sweet. Have no fear of sudden disaster or of the ruin that overtakes the wicked, for the Lord will be at your side and will keep your foot from being snared" (Proverbs 3:21-26).

Foreword

I don't think I'm exaggerating when I say that our nation has, in just a few years, given itself to "gross darkness." When I was a child, I didn't have the temptations that this generation has, because I didn't have the opportunity to feed my sinful heart. It took some effort to get hold of an explicit picture. But nowadays, children can be swallowed into a whirlpool of filth in a matter of seconds, and our sinful natures don't resist for a second. We drink iniquity like water. Without a solid biblical knowledge of God that produces a healthy fear of the Lord, this generation cannot survive. God bless Gregg Jackson for his passion to see that children are trained up in the way they should go. Without godly instruction, this godless generation is heading for eternal destruction in a very real Hell. May this book be divinely used to raise a generation of men and women who will have the boldness of Elijah, the faith of Abraham, the courage of David, the wisdom of Solomon, and the passion of Paul—and may all of what they do for the Kingdom of God be motivated by the love of Christ… for love is the fountain of all that we do."

—Ray Comfort, author and cohost, *The Way of the Master*

Introduction

Freedom is never more than one generation away from extinction. We didn't pass it to our children in the bloodstream. It must be fought for, protected, and handed on for them to do the same, or one day we will spend our sunset years telling our children and our children's children what it was once like in the United States, where men were free.
　　　　　　　—President Ronald W. Reagan

One of my greatest burdens and desires as a father is for my eight-year-old son to grow up honoring God with his life, knowing right from wrong, and acting on that knowledge. I am far more interested in his character than I am in which college he attends or his profession. I am sure that I am not alone.

In fact, if you are reading these words, you too must possess that same burden and sense of obligation that I do, to pass on the same truths that have guided the best parts of your life to your children, so that they may know the truth, and that their lives will glorify God.

During most of American history, when a biblical worldview prevailed, much of the information in this book was common knowledge, even among non-Christians. But we live in a day where "good has become evil and evil good," where "everyone does what is right in his own eyes." A time when quoting God's Word in public can literally get you arrested for a "hate crime."

And that is precisely why I am writing this book—to arm you, the parent, with what I believe to be among the most important biblical truths that we can pass on to the next generation, the stuff that they are never going to learn in most schools, from the media, and sadly, in many churches.

These are the types of things they must understand and apply if they have any hope of living a life of faith in an increasingly dark cultural and spiritual climate, the most important truths that I would share with my son if I were on my deathbed.

My sincere hope and prayer is that Christian parents share this politically incorrect book with their children so that the next generation may be adequately prepared to defend biblical truth for the advancement of the Gospel and biblical truth in general—the only real antidote for what really ails America and the rest of the world.

—In Jesus' Name, Gregg Jackson

Chapter 1
Seek First the Kingdom

The world will tell you to "look out for number one" and to seek your own happiness in life. But the Bible says the exact opposite. God says, "*Seek first the Kingdom and His righteousness and all other things will be added unto you*" (Matthew 6:33). You see, while you may be quite near the center of the universe, you are not the center of the universe. God is. And one of the main reasons He created you, is to glorify Him through our worship and relationship with Him, and by extension, others. God made the universe, the earth, and people like us so He could have someone to talk to, someone to do things with, and someone to love. He is the most famous and talked-about person in all history. The Bible says that God's fame is a part of His "glory." And when you talk to God, and give God His rightful place as your leader in life, you bring Him even greater glory (and you make Him happy)! God has promised those who are His children that, when we place our faith in Him and make His Son Jesus our Lord and Savior, He will add everything else that we need in our lives, and that He will give us above and beyond what we could ever imagine. When you delight yourself in the LORD, He will give you the desires of your heart (Psalm 37:4).

Chapter 2
You Were Created by God

The world will tell you that you are nothing more than matter and energy and that you "evolved" from animals. You are not an animal. Nor did you "evolve" from one. God created the heavens and the earth and created the first human, Adam, on the sixth day of Creation Week. God created you in His very image and you are totally distinct from any other person ever to inhabit the earth: "*So God created mankind in his own image, in the image of God he created them; male and female he created them*"(Genesis 1:27). He also knew you before anyone else would see you, or even knew you were alive. "*Before I formed you in the womb I knew you, before you were born I set you apart*" (Jeremiah 1:5). Don't ever doubt that God made you and loves you so much that He put on human flesh and came to earth to die for you. You are His child. "*I praise you because I am fearfully and wonderfully made; your works are wonderful, I know that full well*" (Psalm 139:14).

Chapter 3
The Bible Is God's Truth

The world will claim that the Bible is just a mythical book of stories and that it can't be trusted as the ultimate source of truth that Christians claim it is. A number of reasons exist, however, as to why we can trust the Bible to be the inspired Word of God. First, God Himself declares it to be true: *"Every word of God is flawless; he is a shield to those who take refuge in him"* (Proverbs 30:5). There are also more original copies of the Bible than of any other literary work in history. The ancient texts from which God's Word originated have a remarkable consistency and cohesion to one another. Moreover, an abundance of archeological evidence has confirmed many of the historical and cultural references in the Bible. The Bible was also written over a 1,500-year period by 40 different authors—the vast majority of whom were martyred for their faith. Would you die for something you knew to be a lie? Finally, Jesus fulfilled 351 individual Biblical prophecies. The mathematical probability of one man fulfilling only eight of these prophecies is about 10 to the 17th power, or one-in 100,000,000,000,000,000… A number so large, that it would be equivalent to laying silver dollars two feet deep on the face of the state of Texas, marking only one of them, and having a blindfolded man pick the marked silver dollar—statistically impossible! The fact that one Man, the God-man Jesus Christ, God the Son, fulfilled all 351 individual biblical prophesies is the only proof we really need that Jesus is who He claimed to be, and that the Bible is the infallible and authoritative Divinely Revealed Word of God. But if that isn't convincing enough, I can promise you that if you authentically pray that God would reveal Himself to you as you read it, He promises that He will.

Chapter 4
Jesus Is the Only Way to Heaven

The world will say that "there are many roads to heaven." And that all religions are basically the same. They will claim that if your good deeds outweigh your bad deeds, you will end up in heaven (if they even believe that such a place exists). The Bible however, says the exact opposite. Jesus said: *"I am the way, the truth and the life. No one comes to the Father except through me"* (John 14:6). Faith alone, in Christ alone, by God's grace alone, is the only way to have your sins forgiven and be granted eternal life in heaven. God loves you so much that He made it explicitly clear in the Scriptures, so we would not be confused. Because God is not the author of confusion, there is but one way to Heaven…through faith in Jesus alone!

Chapter 5
You Are Not "Basically Good"

The world says man is basically good but God says that man's heart is *"deceitful above all things and beyond cure"* (Jeremiah 17:9), and that we are all born with a sinful nature (a tendency to do what is wrong). While people may do good works and act morally, God says those "good works" are like "filthy rags" to Him. Only God is perfectly good, and the only true righteousness we ever possess during our lives is when we invite Jesus into our hearts to be our Lord and Savior. When that happens, He gives us a spiritual heart transplant and a new birth. The Bible says that all things become new when we place our faith in Him. And the good things that we actually do are not done to earn our salvation. They are works that God Himself created for us to walk in once we are saved to please and glorify Him, and to provide a testimony to other unbelievers that our faith in the One true God of the universe is real.

Chapter 6
Your Life Began at Conception

The world says that life begins at "viability," or "implantation" or even birth, and that until you grew large enough to meet one of these definitions, you were just a "blob of cells." But God says that He knew you when you were being formed in your mother's womb: *"For you formed my inward parts. You wove me in my mother's womb. I will give thanks to you for I am fearfully and wonderfully made"* (Psalm 139:14). All human beings are made in the very image of God and possess a God-given (inalienable) right to life from the very moment they become living human beings—at the very moment they are conceived, when the male sperm inseminates the female egg (ovum). The Word of God clearly states that life begins at conception (Job 31:15, Isaiah 49:1, Jeremiah 1:5, Psalm 139:13-16) and that unborn life is still life. For example, a pregnant Mary is told by Elizabeth that the baby in her womb (Jesus' cousin John the Baptist) "leapt for joy" when Mary arrived with the baby Jesus in her womb (Luke 1:39-44). In the Mosaic Law there were penalties for even accidentally killing an unborn person (Exodus 21:22-25). In church tradition, one of the oldest known summaries of teachings is called *The Didache,* and it includes the line "you shall not murder a child by abortion nor kill them when they're born."

Chapter 7
God Created and Defined Marriage

The world says that marriage is whatever the majority of voters say it is, but God says that He created marriage, which is between a male and a female. What God has defined can never be redefined by man: *"For this reason a man shall leave his father and his mother and be joined to his wife and they shall become one flesh"* (Genesis 2:24). That is God's plan for marriage and the natural human family.

Chapter 8
God Created the Heavens and the Earth in Six Literal Days

The world says that the earth came into being spontaneously, and by chance, from a random "Big Bang" and that animals and even people are the result of "biological evolution." But God says in the very first words of the Bible that He created the heavens and the earth: *"In the beginning God created the heavens and the earth"* (Genesis 1:1). Our eternally existing God literally breathed His creation into being in six literal 24-hour days, and rested on the seventh. It is impossible for something to come from nothing. That is called magic. And magic is not real. It is just an illusion. But the God of the Bible is real. He is the Creator of the heavens and the earth!

Chapter 9
The Earth Is As Old As the Bible Says It Is

The world says that the earth is four or five billion years old, and that the entire universe is some 16 billion years old. But the Bible indicates that the earth is less than 10,000 years old. While nobody was actually present at Creation, numerous scientific discoveries have provided evidence for a "young earth," in accordance with the biblical account of Creation, and the written genealogies of the Bible. The book of Genesis is not a mythological or poetic book, as many claim. Genesis is the first book of the first five books of the Bible also known as the "Torah," or "The Law." All of the Scripture writers and Jesus Himself all believed Genesis to be a literal historical account of Creation. Genesis is not written in a poetic style that we find often in the book of Psalms for example, rather it is written as an historical narrative.

Chapter 10
Man and Dinosaurs Were Both Created on the Sixth Day

The world says that dinosaurs predated humans by "millions of years." But the Bible says, and science has confirmed, that man and dinosaurs coexisted and were both created on the sixth day of Creation Week: "*And God said, Let the earth bring forth the living creature after his kind, cattle, and creeping thing, and beast of the earth after his kind: and it was so. And God made the beast of the earth after his kind, and cattle after their kind, and everything that creepeth upon the earth after his kind: and God saw that it was good. And God said, Let us make man in our image, after our likeness: and let them have dominion over the fish of the sea, and over the fowl of the air, and over the cattle, and over all the earth, and over every creeping thing that creepeth upon the earth. So God created man in his own image, in the image of God created he him; male and female created he them*" (Genesis 1:24-27). Also, the very word "dinosaur" was not even invented until 1858, ten years after the publication of Charles Darwin's *Origin of Species*. For all of human history prior to 1858, "dinosaurs" were called "dragons," even in the Bible. In the Book of Job, for example, Job describes a "behemoth:" "*Behold now behemoth, which I made with thee; he eateth grass as an ox.*

Lo now, his strength is in his loins, and his force is in the navel of his belly. He moveth his tail like a cedar: the sinews of his stones are wrapped together. His bones are as strong pieces of brass; his bones are like bars of iron" (Job 40:15-18). Most biblical commentators believe that the word "behemoth" describes a very large dinosaur-like animal.

Furthermore, a significant amount of scientific fossil evidence shows "dinosaurs" to be thousands (not millions) of years old, and that many—perhaps even all—of the largest died after the Flood, due to environmental reasons. Many scientific journals are reporting amazing discoveries of original biological material that grew within dinosaurs! Biological remains from an extinct bird and an extinct reptile (an *Archaeopteryx* and a mosasaur), and even actual discoveries of dinosaur soft tissue, are being reported by many of the most famous scientific journals, including *Nature, Science,* the *Proceedings of the National Academy of Sciences, Public Library of Science, Proceedings of the Royal Society, Bone,* and the *Journal of Vertebrate Paleontology.*

The biological material that scientists have discovered so far in dinosaur fossils, and from these other fossils in similar rock layers, includes blood vessels, red blood cells, different proteins (including collagen and hemoglobin), and even decomposing dinosaur DNA! Also contained within these fossils are the kinds of atoms and amino acids that cannot last millions of years, but only thousands of years. All these discoveries are similar to what we find in Egyptian mummies of people who died about 4,000 years ago. Yet this soft tissue has survived in the fossils of various extinct animals and even from six species of dinosaurs, which is strong scientific evidence that they did not die out millions of years ago, but thousands. So far, the dinosaurs discovered with surviving biological material in their fossils are *Hadrosaurus*, the titanosaur, the ornithomimosaur (an ostrich-like dinosaur), *Triceratops, Lufengosaurus* (one of the smaller long-necked dinosaurs), and even the fierce-looking *Tyrannosaurus rex*. Scientists from North Carolina State University even found soft, flexible, and transparent blood vessels from a *T. rex*.

Chapter 11
Noah's Flood Was Worldwide

The world says that Noah's flood was just a regional occurrence, if it happened at all, and that there was never a global flood. But the Bible clearly states that the flood was worldwide: "*Then the flood came upon the earth for forty days and the water increased and lifted up the ark so it rose above the earth*" (Genesis 7:17). The Bible is explicitly clear when it states that "*the waters prevailed exceedingly upon the earth and all the high hills that were under the whole heaven were covered*" (Genesis 7:19). Furthermore, we are also told that after the Flood, the "*earth was divided*" (Genesis 10:25), which may explain why, if you carefully study the shapes of the continents, they seem to fit together perfectly! Historical accounts from all around the world and other scientific evidence also strongly support the biblical account of a global flood. Perhaps the strongest evidence in support of a global flood however, is this: Since the time God promised Noah that He would never again flood the *earth*, thousands of *regional* floods have taken place. So, if indeed Noah's flood was "regional," as the world claims, then God's promise would have been a lie. And God does not lie.

Chapter 12
One Man with God Makes a Majority

The world says that the majority rules. But what if what the majority wants to do is evil in the eyes of the Lord? You have an obligation to stand in the minority, even if you are the only one to oppose any ideas, policies or laws that are contrary to what God has established to be wrong in His Divinely Revealed Word. You will probably be persecuted for your principled position, and ridiculed for not going along with the crowd, but know that when you stand for what is right according to God's Word, you are always standing with God, and are therefore always in the majority. God is much, much bigger than any group of men. In fact, God alone *is* a majority, and you will be wise to follow Him.

Chapter 13
You Work for God, Not Man!

The world may tell you that you have to bend the rules or do something unethical once in a while to get ahead of the competition, but you ultimately work for God if you are one of His children, and everything you do in your job, should ultimately be done to please God. Even if your boss and co-workers may not be watching you. Remember, God is. God is Jehova Roi (the God who sees). *So whether you eat or drink or whatever you do, do it all for the glory of God* (1 Corinthians 10:31).

Chapter 14
Fear God, Not Man!

A spirit of fear seems to prevail these days. But know with 100 percent certainty that God has not given you a spirit of fear "*but of power, and of love and of a sound mind*" (2 Timothy 1:7). The Bible also says that the "*fear of man will prove to be a snare, but whoever trusts in the LORD is kept safe*" (Proverbs 29:25). When you have the God of the Universe on your side, you never have to be fearful of any person or situation. God has promised that He will never leave you nor forsake you. The Bible also says that "*to hate evil is to fear God*" (Proverbs 8:13). When we hate the things that God hates, we are demonstrating a healthy awe, reverence, and fear of God. The closer you draw to God and trust in Him, the more rapidly your fears will dissipate! "*No one will be able to stand against you all the days of your life. As I was with Moses, so I will be with you; I will never leave you nor forsake you. Be strong and courageous, because you will lead these people to inherit the land I swore to their ancestors to give them. Be strong and very courageous. Be careful to obey all the law my servant Moses gave you; do not turn from it to the right or to the left, that you may be successful wherever you go. Keep this Book of the Law always on your lips; meditate on it day and night, so that you may be careful to do everything written in it. Then you will be prosperous and success-ful. Have I not commanded you? Be strong and courageous. Do not be afraid; do not be discouraged, for the* Lord *your God will be with you wherever you go"* (Joshua 1:5-9).

Chapter 15
Be Quick to Listen and Slow to Speak

It seems as if almost everybody these days is quick to have their opinions known to the world on a whole host of topics via social media. And while you should never be afraid to share yours, regardless of how politically incorrect they may be, it is vital that you always remember that God gave you two ears and one mouth for a reason. The Bible says that the *"The tongue has the power of life and death, and those who love it will eat its fruit"* (Proverbs 18:21). Take time before providing your "two cents," especially if the conversation gets heated. And remember that once something is said, it is very hard to take it back. Choose your words wisely and consider how what you say may affect others; ask yourself if God would approve of what you are about to say or write. That is always a good test.

Chapter 16
Judge Righteously

The world says we should never judge other people. But God says to judge righteously. While we are never to judge hypocritically by jumping to conclusions about people based on their outward appearance only, we are commanded to judge people "by their fruit" (i.e., by what they say and do): *"Do not judge according to appearance, but judge with righteous judgment"* (John 7:24). God has given you a brain and an ability to judge (to distinguish right from wrong, danger from safety, truth from lies, etc.); in fact, you do it at least a hundred times every day. How many things ought you to judge, you ask? Well, God's Word tells us that *"the spiritual man judges all things."* (1 Corinthians 2:15). Choose your friends wisely: *"Do not be misled: Bad company corrupts good character"* (1 Corinthians 15:33). Pray to God that His Holy Spirit will help guide and direct you to judge *righteously* and not hypocritically.

Chapter 17
God's Wisdom Is Greater Than Man's

The world says that those who base their beliefs on God's Word are narrow-minded "Bible thumpers." They will say that it was just a book written long ago by a bunch of delusional men, that humanity has greatly evolved since then, and that what the Bible has to say is outdated. Nonsense! The Bible is the number-one bestseller of all time for a reason. Its God-breathed, God-inspired truths are timeless: *"The Word of the Lord remains forever"* (Isaiah 40:8). God's Word is the *"sword of the spirit"* (Ephesians 6:17). *"Living and active, sharper than any two-edged sword"* (Hebrews 4:12). *"Every word of God proves true"* (Proverbs 30:5). *"In the beginning was the Word and the Word was with God and the Word was God. He was in the beginning with God. All things were made through Him and without Him nothing was made that was made"* (John 1:1-3). *"And the Word became flesh (in the human body of Jesus)"* (John 1:14). The apostle Paul commands us to "let the word of Christ dwell in you richly" (Colossians 3:16) (by reading His Word in the Bible!). No matter how smart we may think we are, all worldly wisdom pales in comparison to the wisdom of the Word of Almighty God. May it encourage and strengthen you, and guide and direct your steps in this life, in preparation for the eternal one to come. Begin and finish every day in His Word!

Chapter 18
Forgive as You
Have Been Forgiven

If you are a Christian, God has forgiven you for all your sins (past, present, and future) and given you eternal life. Even though we continue to sin after we are saved, God's Word tells us that *when we acknowledge our sins "he is just and faithful to forgive them."* (1 John 1:9). When Jesus was being crucified by those who hated Him, He said, *"Father, forgive them, for they know not what they do"* (Luke 23:34). Likewise, we as believers, who have experienced the ultimate forgiveness of all our sins, should be quick to forgive others when they genuinely acknowledge their sins. In doing so, we are demonstrating God's mercy to them. God promises us that when we forgive others, we too will experience the refreshment of His peace and forgiveness (Luke 6:37).

Chapter 19
Don't "Trust Your Heart"

The world will tell you to "trust your heart." But God says that your heart is *"deceitful above all things and beyond all cure"* (Jeremiah 17:9). In other words, oftentimes our heart deceives us—telling us that something is good for us, when in truth it is contrary to God's Word and His will for our lives. The fleshly human heart can often deceive, but when we actively give our heart to Jesus, it's like getting a heart transplant, and He promises to disclose the purposes of our new hearts to us (1 Corinthians 4:5). Don't trust your heart. Trust God's Word to guide and direct you. The world says to "pick yourself up by your bootstraps" and that "God helps those who help themselves." But God says just the opposite. When you encounter difficult times, rely on God. Jesus said, *"Come to me, all you who labor and are heavy laden and I will give you rest. Take my yoke upon you and learn from me, for I am gentle and lowly in heart and you will find rest for your souls. For my yoke is easy and my burden is light"* (Matthew 11:28-30). The more you try to do things in your own power without relying on the Lord, the more trouble you will have in this life. God has designed us to be in a relationship with Him and to abide in Him, and to trust Him fully with our lives…To allow Him to become our lives! Jesus said, *"I am the vine. You are the branches. Whoever abides in Me and I in him will bear much fruit. For apart from me you can do nothing"* (John 15:5). Don't trust in yourself. Instead, *"trust in the Lord and lean not on your own understanding. But in all your ways acknowledge Him and He will make your paths straight"* (Proverbs 3:5-6).

Chapter 20
You Are Called to Be Sexually Pure

The world will tell you that having sexual relationships prior to getting married is acceptable and even beneficial. But the truth is that God has specifically called you to be pure, and to not engage in sexual relations prior to marriage (i.e., to engage in fornication): *"Flee from sexual immorality. All other sins a man commits are outside his body, but he who sins sexually sins against his own body. Do you not know that your body is a temple of the Holy Spirit, who is in you, whom you have received from God? You are not your own; you were bought at a price. Therefore honor God with your body"* (1 Cor 6:18-20). If you want to be *assured* of God's blessings, anointing, and hand over your life, honor Him with your body (sexuality)! Your sexuality should be reserved only for your future wife (*or husband in case of daughter*). This is God's *promise* of blessing upon your life, your marriage, your future, and your children's lives: *"Therefore, I urge you, brothers, in view of God's mercy, to offer your bodies as living sacrifices, holy and pleasing to God—this is your spiritual act of worship. Do not conform any longer to the pattern of this world, but be transformed by the renewing of your mind. Then you will be able to test and approve what God's will is-- his good, pleasing and perfect will"* (Rom 12:1-2).

Chapter 21
You Are Called to Preach the Gospel!

The world says that you shouldn't talk about "religion," but God says that, as Christians, our primary duty in this life is to share the Good News (i.e., the Gospel of Jesus' life, death, and resurrection) with everybody we encounter in life: *"Go therefore and make disciples of all nations, baptizing them in the name of the Father and of the Son and of the Holy Spirit teaching them to observe all that I have commanded you."* (Matthew 28:19) If we truly love people, we will share with them the eternal truth that *"God so loved the world, He gave His only Son, that whoever believes in Him should not perish but have eternal life."* (John 3:16)

Chapter 22
You Should Be Narrow-Minded!

The world will say that you should not be narrow-minded, and that you must be "tolerant" of all beliefs, because there isn't just one "right" way. Everybody has to decide for themselves what is right. But God says, *"Enter through the narrow gate. For wide is the gate and broad is the road that leads to destruction, and many enter through it. But small is the gate and narrow the road that leads to life, and only a few find it"* (Matthew 7:13-14.) God's Word alone is the basis for all truth. You may be ridiculed, or even persecuted for basing your values, beliefs, and decisions in life firmly on God's authoritative and inerrant Word, but remember that the One True God has called you to be narrow-minded, and to enter through the Narrow Gate—Jesus Himself!

Chapter 23
You Are Called to be
a Seed-Planter

You are not God. Only God's Holy Spirit can ultimately convict a sinner of his sin and need of a savior. You will encounter many people in your life who desperately need Jesus, but who are not saved, and it will make you feel sad at times. Share the truth of who Jesus is and what He has done in your life with them, and pray for your un-saved family and friends. Just know that, ultimately, each individual has to make a decision for himself as to whether he will accept or reject the free gift of salvation that only Jesus offers. Your job in life isn't to save people, rather to let them know that they can be forgiven of all their sins, and receive eternal life by acknowledging their sins, and placing their faith in Jesus. That's what obedient children of the Living, Loving God of Heaven do! They plant seeds of truth and let God provide for the increase, and God's Holy Spirit ultimately convicts a sinner's heart to repent: *"But how can they call on him unless they believe in him? And how can they believe in him if they have never heard about him? And how can they hear about him unless someone tells them? And how will anyone go and tell them without being sent? That is why the Scriptures say, 'How beautiful are the feet of messengers who bring good news!"* (Romans 10:14-15)

Chapter 24
Duty Is Ours;
Results Are God's

God has not called you to be successful. He has called you to love Him. And this is, in large part, what having faith is: loving and obeying God, even when you can't clearly see the purpose or outcome. There will be many times during your life when you will be encouraged to do certain things that you know are not right in order to achieve some stated "good" outcome. God cares more about our obedience than about the results we achieve. God doesn't need us taking shortcuts for Him to achieve His sovereign will and purposes in our lives. Peter and the Apostles were once told not to preach the name of Jesus. They responded, *"We must obey God rather than men"* (Acts 5:29). Indeed, it is far more important to obey God, regardless of the cost, and allow Him to determine the results.

Chapter 25

Thanksgiving, Christmas, and Easter Are About Much More Than Turkey, Presents, and Chocolate Eggs

The world may think that Thanksgiving is about dinner celebrations with family and friends and watching football, but Thanksgiving is an Annual Day of Thanks to God Almighty for His blessings and Mercies. Governor William Bradford of the Pilgrim colony called the "Plymouth Plantation" in Plymouth, Massachusetts established Thanksgiving in 1620. Bradford, a devout Christian, proclaimed: "All ye Pilgrims with your wives and little ones, do gather at the Meeting House, on the hill... there to listen to the pastor, and render Thanksgiving to the Almighty God for all His blessings." On November 1, 1777, by an order of Congress, the first National Thanksgiving Proclamation was issued, and signed by Henry Laurens, President of the Continental Congress. The third Thursday of December 1777 was thus officially set aside "... for solemn thanksgiving and praise. That with one heart and one voice the good people may express the grateful feelings of their hearts, and consecrate themselves to the service of their

Divine Benefactor; ... and their humble and earnest supplication that it may please God, through the merits of Jesus Christ, mercifully to forgive and blot (their manifold sins) out of remembrance..." On January 1, 1795, our first United States President, George Washington, wrote his famed National Thanksgiving Proclamation, in which he said that it is... "... our duty as a people, with devout reverence and affectionate gratitude, to acknowledge our many and great obligations to Almighty God, and to implore Him to continue and confirm the blessings we experienced..." Many years later, on October 3, 1863, Abraham Lincoln proclaimed, by an Act of Congress, an annual National Day of Thanksgiving "on the last Thursday of November, as a day of Thanksgiving and Praise to our beneficent Father who dwelleth in the heavens."

Christmas is about much more than presents. While the world has made Christmas into a materialistic secular event that celebrates general "peace," don't ever forget that Christmas marks the day that *real* peace, God's peace, came to earth, in the person of Jesus Christ our Savior, the Son of the Living God, who was born to ultimately lay down His life, so that those who repent of their sins and place their faith in Him may be forgiven and have eternal life with Him in Heaven. While Christmas is a time we give and receive gifts with our family and friends, never forget that the greatest gift you will ever receive in this lifetime, is the gift of salvation and eternal life that only Jesus provides!

Easter is about much more than chocolate eggs. Like Christmas, Easter has also become an overtly secular event. Never forget however, that Easter is a holy day that commemorates the day Jesus rose from the dead and ascended into heaven. Easter Sunday is really Resurrection Sunday! Christianity is true because the tomb in which our Lord Jesus was buried, was empty! The empty tomb is probably the greatest and most authenticated event in human history! The Apostle Paul said that if Christ never rose from the dead, then Christianity would be false, and our faith in vain: *"And if Christ has not been raised, then our preaching is vain, your faith also is vain"*(1 Corinthians 15:14). But He did rise from the dead, and we who believe in Him become new creations as we also die with Him and are raised with Him! *"Therefore, if anyone is in Christ, he is a new creation. The old has passed away; behold, the new has come"* (2 Corinthians 5:17).

Chapter 26
God Has Many Names!

People may tell you that "God *is* Love." And while God is Love, the one true God of the Bible has more than 200 names, and when you include all the nicknames and titles, there are actually more than 700 names! The Bible tells us that "*those who know your name put their trust in you*" (Psalm 9:10). If you desire to have an intimate relationship with God and to grow in your faith, familiarize yourself with His many names. Here are a few of them:

- *Elohim*: "Strong Creator"

- Jehova, Yahweh, I Am: Self-Existing, Unchanging

- *El Kana*: "Jealous God"

- *El Elyon*: "The Most High"

- *El Shaddai*: "God Almighty"

- *Jehova-El Emeth*: "The Lord God of Truth"

- *Adonai*: "Lord"

- *El Roi*: "The God Who Sees"

- *Jehovah-Or*: "The Lord Is Light"

- *Jehova-Shammah*: "The Lord Is There"

- *Jehova-Sabaoth*: "The Lord of Hosts"

- *Jehova-Jireh*: "The Lord Will Provide"

- *Jehova-Shalom*: "The Lord of Peace"

- *Jehova-Maginnenu*: "The Lord Our Defense"

- *Jehova-Rohi*: "The Lord My Shepherd"

- Messiah

- Salvation in No Other Name

- Coming King

- Father

- Helper

- Overcomer

Chapter 27
Glorify God by How You Handle Your Money

The world will tell you that money is evil, but the Bible says that money itself is not evil, rather: *"love of money that is the root of all evil"* (1 Timothy 6:10). Money itself is not evil. Webster's Dictionary defines money as: "something generally accepted as a medium of exchange, a measure of value, or a means of payment for goods and services." You should work hard in your life and use the money you earn to support yourself and your family. The Bible says, *"The soul of the sluggard craves and gets nothing, while the soul of the diligent is richly supplied"* (Proverbs 13:4), and that *"... If anyone is not willing to work, let him not eat. For we hear that some among you walk in idleness, not busy at work, but busybodies. Now such persons we command and encourage in the Lord Jesus Christ to do their work quietly and to earn their own living"* (2 Thessalonians: 10-12), and that *"if anyone does not provide for his relatives, and especially for members of his household, he has denied the faith and is worse than an unbeliever"* (1 Timothy 5:8). You should also offer a portion of your earnings to support the church to which you belong, and to other Christian-based ministries that proclaim the Gospel and help the orphan and the widow in need: *"Honor the LORD with your wealth, with the firstfruits of all your crops"* (Proverbs 3:9). You will find that, when you use your money for the things of the Lord, He will provide everything else that you need in your life. The world will constantly tell you that you need to buy this or that thing now and to "live for today." The Bible says however, that a wise man saves for the future and his family: *"Precious treasure and oil are in a wise man's dwelling, but a foolish man devours it"* (Proverbs 21:20), and that *"A good man leaves an inheritance to his children's children, but the sinner's wealth is laid up for the righteous"* (Proverbs 13:22). You are called to be a good steward of the money with which God blesses you. May you glorify the Lord mightily in how you choose to handle your finances!

Chapter 28
The "Lesser of Two Evils" Is Still Evil!

The world says that we must choose the "lesser of two evils" when faced with two imperfect choices. But God says that we *must never do evil that good may come of it* (Romans 3:8). Charles Spurgeon, the most famous theologian of the last 300 years, famously said, "When faced with two evils, choose neither." While you may be ridiculed for not going along with the crowd, or for not supporting the "lesser of two evils," you can sleep soundly with a clear conscience knowing that when you stand with God in opposition to all evil, you are always acting in obedience to Him: *Blessed are those who keep his testimonies, who seek him with their whole heart* (Psalm 119:2).

Chapter 29
God Created
"Mother Nature"

The world talks about "Mother Nature" when they talk about the weather. That term is a euphemism for God… The God of the Bible. God created the universe and set the weather in motion. God created the heavens and the earth and is all-powerful and totally sovereign. While man may attempt to manipulate the weather, only God is sovereign over it. The earth's temperature and climate is always changing (getting cooler/warmer) primarily due to the sun, and not human activity.

Chapter 30
We Are Not "Evolving"; We Are Devolving

The world says that society continues to evolve and progress. But the Bible says the opposite. Sin entered the world through Adam's first act of disobedience in The Garden of Eden, resulting in death and suffering. The earth as we know it is dying out (devolving) until the day when it is burned up and is replaced by the new heaven and a new earth: "*But the day of the Lord will come like a thief. The heavens will disappear with a roar; the elements will be destroyed by fire, and the earth and everything done in it will be laid bare*" (2 Peter 3:10). Many will tell you that society must accommodate the changing traditions and behaviors of men. But God's Word never changes (or "evolves"), because God is the same yesterday, today, and tomorrow.

Chapter 31
God Has Defined Right and Wrong

The world says that society determines standards of right and wrong by consensus and majority vote. God says the exact opposite. He alone sets standards of right and wrong. His Divinely Revealed Word is the transcendent moral authority on all issues. The definitions of the words "good" and "evil" must not be left up to the imaginations of imperfect and sinful men. Only God has the right to define the words "good" and "evil," and men must comport with His unchanging definition of the concepts given both implicitly and explicitly in the Ten Commandments. Any law or court opinion contrary to the Supreme Law of the Land, the United States Constitution, and God's Divinely Revealed Word is legally null and void:

- St. Thomas Aquinas: *"Any law contrary to God's Law is no law at all."*

- St. Peter: *"We must obey God rather than man."*

- Sir William Blackstone: *"No enactment of man can be considered law unless it conforms to the law of God."*

- Samuel Rutherford, in *Lex, Rex*: *"There is a transcendent fixed rule of law that must govern man and societies."*

Chapter 32
There Is Only One Race of People: The Human Race!

The world says there are many different races and constantly tries to separate people based on their skin color, but the Bible says that there is only one race—the Human Race—and different groups of people. Every person on this earth has two common ancestors—Adam and Eve. According to the Human Genome Project, there are no such things as biological races of people. Furthermore, do not be deceived by evolutionary theory that the "more evolved" white race is superior to darker skin color races. This is the racist foundational philosophy behind Fascism, Nazism, and Marxism. In the end, there are really only two types of people: those who are saved by the blood of Jesus and those who aren't.

Chapter 33
Christians Founded America and Our Laws Were Based on the Bible

You will be told that America is a secular nation and "no longer a Christian nation." That is a lie. America's first settlers (the Puritans and Pilgrims) came to the "New World" (as they called it) to freely worship Jesus. They fled from England, where their worship was highly regulated by the King. The overwhelming majority of our nation's first settlers were devout, born-again, Bible-believing Christians. The opening sentence of the New England Confederation, written by Puritans, reads, "We came into these parts of America with one and the same end, namely, to advance the Kingdom of the Lord Jesus Christ." And our Founding documents, including the Mayflower Compact, the Declaration of Independence, and the Constitution, were based largely on the Bible. The Supreme Court (in *Church of the Holy Trinity v. United States*) has even acknowledged that we are a "Christian nation." Our founding national charter, and part of the Organic Law of the United States, the Declaration of Independence proclaims that "[Men] are endowed by their Creator with certain unalienable Rights, that among these are Life, Liberty and the pursuit of Happiness." The document also says that these rights are "self-evident" and that they constitute the "Laws of Nature." These principles are taken directly from the Bible.

Chapter 34
There Is No "Separation of Church and State" in Our Constitution

You will be told that religion and politics don't mix and must be kept separate because our Constitution calls for the "separation of church and state." Problem is, there is no "separation of church and state" in our Constitution. God is sovereign over civil matters and governments are instituted among men to protect and defend God-given (inalienable) rights. You can't have a virtuous and moral government without virtuous and moral people who fear God and obey His Word. Founding Father James Madison said as much in Federalist #51: "... But what is government itself, but the greatest of all reflections on human nature? If men were angels, no government would be necessary. If angels were to govern men, neither external nor internal controls on government would be necessary." You can't separate the Christian values from civil government. Thus you can't separate the Christian religion from civil government.

Chapter 35

The Main Function of Biblical Government Is to Reward the Righteous and Punish the Wicked (Romans 13)

You will be told that government exists to provide healthcare and welfare for the poor and to generally "spread the wealth." Not true. The primary purpose of civil government is to protect God-given rights by ensuring justice for the innocent, especially the rights to life, liberty, and private property. Your right to your own life, to protect and defend yourself, your family, and your property, as well as your right to freely assemble to worship God, to criticize the government, to pursue happiness, and to preach the Gospel are God-given rights that no man may grant or take away! Government exists to secure these God-given rights! Any civil magistrate at any level or branch of government who fails to protect and defend these God-given inalienable rights is in violation of his oath and should be removed from office. Additionally you have a duty to oppose and expose any such enemies of liberty and freedom!

Chapter 36
You Reap What You Sow Here on Earth and in Heaven

The world speaks of *karma* (the idea that the way in which you live your life now will influence the type of life you have when you are reincarnated). The entire concept of *karma* is based on the polytheistic religion of Hinduism, which teaches the way in which you live this life will determine the type of body you are born into in the next. The Bible teaches the exact opposite. The Bible rejects the notion of reincarnation and teaches that *"Just as man is destined to die once, and after that to face judgment…"* (Hebrews 9:27). You are only born once and then face judgment. There are no second chances to get it right. Either you repent of your sins in this life and accept the free gift of salvation only found in Jesus and go to heaven forever, or reject the free gift of salvation and spend eternity separated from Him in hell.

Chapter 37
Nobody Is a Lost Cause

Some may claim that this or that person is a "lost cause." But just remember that where there is life, there is hope. God loves all of His creation and desires that we all come to repentance and place our faith in Him: "*The Lord is not slow in keeping his promise, as some understand slowness. Instead he is patient with you, not wanting anyone to perish, but everyone to come to repentance*" (2 Peter 3:9).

Chapter 38
You Can Never
Lose Your Salvation

Some self-professing Christians will tell you that you can lose your salvation and that keeping your salvation depends on how you act in this life. But God's Holy and Authoritative Word says just the opposite. You had nothing to do with your salvation, because it was a free gift that God gave to you by His Divine Mercy and Love. Your free gift of salvation was just that… free! The Bible clearly states that once we acknowledge that we are sinners separated from God by our sin and place our faith in the Lord Jesus Christ, He cleanses us from all of our sins and grants us eternal life with Him in heaven forever. Our salvation has nothing to do with our own efforts or works: *"It is by grace you were saved by faith. Not by works lest any man should boast"* (Ephesians 2:8-9). God's Word is clear that once you place your faith in Jesus, you are saved forever: *"My sheep hear my voice and they follow Me. I give them eternal life and they will never perish, and no one will snatch them out of my hand. My Father who has given them to me is greater than all, and no one is able to snatch them out of the Father's hand. I and the Father are one"* (John 10:27-30). I know of no greater truth!

Chapter 39
Truth Is Not Relative

You will be told that there is no such thing as absolute truth, that "What may be true for you may not be true for somebody else," but that isn't true. In fact you should ask them just once: "is that absolutely true?" You see the very claim that "there is no such thing as absolute truth" is in itself, an absolute statement that contradicts the claim! There is indeed such a thing as absolute truth. And the basis of everything that is true in life can be found in God's Divinely Revealed Word...the Holy Bible. Jesus said it best. "*Sanctify them by the truth; your word is truth*" (John 17:17).

Chapter 40

The Most Important Thing in This Life Is Where You Will Spend Eternity

You will be told that the most important thing in life is to be happy. Not true. The most important thing in this life is whether or not you have accepted the gift of eternal salvation and forgiveness of sins by placing your faith in the Lord Jesus Christ. We will all die one day, and will either spend eternity with God in Heaven, or spend eternity in hell separated from Him. It's really that simple. Have you accepted Jesus Christ as your Lord and Savior? Do you know with 100 percent certainty that, if you died today, you would spend eternity in Heaven forever? " ... *behold, now is the accepted time; behold, today is the day of salvation*" (2 Corinthians 6:2).

- Everyone needs salvation, because we have all sinned.
  "*No one is righteous—not even one. No one is truly wise; no one is seeking God. All have turned away; all have become useless. No one does good, not a single one*" (Romans 3:10-12).

- The price (or consequence) of sin is death.
  "For the wages of sin is death, but the free gift of God is eternal life through Christ Jesus our Lord" (Romans 6:23).

- Jesus Christ died for our sins.
  "But God showed his great love for us by sending Christ to die for us while we were still sinners" (Romans 5:8).

- We receive salvation and eternal life through faith in Jesus Christ.
  "If you confess with your mouth that Jesus is Lord and believe in your heart that God raised him from the dead, you will be saved. For it is by believing in your heart that you are made right with God, and it is by confessing with your mouth that you are saved ..." For *"everyone who calls on the name of the Lord will be saved"* (Romans 10:9-10, and 13).

- Salvation through Jesus Christ brings us into a relationship of peace with God.
  "Therefore, since we have been made right in God's sight by faith, we have peace with God because of what Jesus Christ our Lord has done for us" (Romans 5:1).

"So now there is no condemnation for those who belong to Christ Jesus" (Romans 8:1).

"And I am convinced that nothing can ever separate us from God's love. Neither death nor life, neither angels nor demons, neither our fears for today nor our worries about tomorrow—not even the powers of hell can separate us from God's love. No power in the sky above or in the earth below—indeed, nothing in all creation will ever be able to separate us from the love of God that is revealed in Christ Jesus our Lord" (Romans 8:38-39).

About the Author

Gregg Jackson is the nationally bestselling author of *Conservative Comebacks to Liberal Lies* and *We Won't Get Fooled Again: Where the Christian Right Went Wrong and How to Make America Right Again.* He is a former radio host on WRKO in Boston and KDAR in Los Angeles, an accomplished speaker who speaks to groups on college campuses nationwide, and a writer whose articles have been published in *The Wall Street Journal, The Washington Times, Human Events,* and Townhall.com. He lives with his beautiful bride of 17 years Annie and 9 year old son (to whom this book is dedicated) Jake in Denver, Colorado.

To contact Gregg Jackson for any media or speaking requests please use:

www.greggjackson.com
gregg.jackson@gmail.com